THE SLICE ON PIZZA

THE DISH ON THE DISH: A HISTORY OF YOUR FAVORITE FOODS

JULIE KNUTSON

Published in the United States of America by Cherry Lake Publishing Group
Ann Arbor, Michigan
www.cherrylakepublishing.com

Reading Adviser: Reading Adviser: Beth Walker Gambro, MS, Ed., Reading Consultant, Yorkville, IL
Photo Credits: © nantonov/iStock.com, cover, 1; © Vershinin/iStock.com, 5; © Christopher Halloran/Shutterstock.com, 6; © Courtesy of the Library of Congress, LC-DIG-ppmsca-70101, 8; © Sofy/Shutterstock.com, 9; © NagornyiSergiy/Shutterstock.com, 10; © Everett Collection/Shutterstock.com, 13; © Vincenzo De Bernardo/Shutterstock.com, 14; © Ruslan Mitin/Shutterstock.com, 16; © Fernando Madeira/Shutterstock.com, 17; © ungvar/Shutterstock.com, 18; © Alessio Orru/Shutterstock.com, 21; © Supitcha McAdam/Shutterstock.com, 23; © MariaKovaleva/Shutterstock.com, 24; © Afanasieva/Shutterstock.com, 27; © filadendron/iStock.com, 28

Copyright © 2022 by Cherry Lake Publishing Group
All rights reserved. No part of this book may be reproduced or utilized in any form or by any means without written permission from the publisher.

Cherry Lake Press is an imprint of Cherry Lake Publishing Group.

Library of Congress Cataloging-in-Publication Data

Names: Knutson, Julie, author.
Title: The slice on pizza / Julie Knutson.
Description: Ann Arbor, Michigan : Cherry Lake Publishing, [2022] | Series: The dish on the dish : a history of your favorite foods | Includes bibliographical references and index. | Audience: Grades 4-6
Identifiers: LCCN 2021006152 (print) | LCCN 2021006153 (ebook) | ISBN 9781534187344 (hardcover) | ISBN 9781534188747 (paperback) | ISBN 9781534190146 (pdf) | ISBN 9781534191549 (ebook)
Subjects: CYAC: Pizza—Juvenile literature. | Cooking. | LCGFT: Cookbooks.
Classification: LCC TX770.P58 K59 2022 (print) | LCC TX770.P58 (ebook) | DDC 641.82/48—dc23
LC record available at https://lccn.loc.gov/2021006152
LC ebook record available at https://lccn.loc.gov/2021006153

Cherry Lake Publishing Group would like to acknowledge the work of the Partnership for 21st Century Learning, a Network of Battelle for Kids. Please visit http://www.battelleforkids.org/networks/p21 for more information.

Printed in the United States of America
Corporate Graphics

ABOUT THE AUTHOR

Julie Knutson is an author who lives in northern Illinois with her husband, son, and border collie. She prefers her pancakes with Nutella and bananas, her pizza "Detroit-style," and her mac 'n' cheese with little green peas.

TABLE OF CONTENTS

CHAPTER 1
First Plating 4

CHAPTER 2
Migrations 12

CHAPTER 3
Evolution and Wild Variations 20

CHAPTER 4
Make Your Own! 26

FASCINATING FACTS 29
TIMELINE 30
FURTHER READING 31
GLOSSARY 32
INDEX 32

CHAPTER 1

First Plating

The Teenage Mutant Ninja Turtles got inventive with it. They created pies like "Beneath These Streets" with licorice and granola and "Green With Jealousy," topped by peanut butter and clams. In Chicago, Illinois, it's a chewy, thick-crusted explosion of cheese. In Iceland and Sweden, it's frequently offered with curried bananas on top. And in Brazil, you might find it sprinkled with green peas or seafood.

It's the global food phenomenon that is . . . PIZZA.

To pizza purists, it's debatable if some of these wild styles even qualify as pizza. But just what exactly is pizza? How do you define it? Is it simply a flatbread with toppings baked into it? If so, the ancient Egyptians, Greeks, and Romans ate it. Is it specifically

Pepperoni is the most popular pizza topping in the United States.

Fruit pizzas are actually pizza-shaped tarts.

leavened bread topped with tomato sauce and cheese? Is a dessert "pizza" with marshmallows and melted chocolate *really* a pizza, or is it a distant cousin?

While the answer depends on who you ask, many food historians see the tomato as the key ingredient that makes a pizza a pizza. This evolution of the flatbread traces to Naples, Italy, in the 17th and 18th centuries. There, it was an inexpensive and simple street food for the city's poor. Then Europe's third-largest city, Naples was densely populated. Many residents lived in cramped spaces with few resources to cook. To meet the need for something filling and portable, street vendors sold flatbreads topped with whatever was available. Many **Neapolitans** ate this bread for breakfast, lunch, and dinner!

The World on a Pie

At quick glance, a Neapolitan pizza seems quite simple. It is tomato sauce, mozzarella, and basil baked to perfection atop a wheat crust. But this specific type of flatbread wouldn't have been possible without the marriage of ingredients from around the world. In the **early modern period**, tomatoes were introduced to Europe from the Americas, first reaching Italy in 1544. This food migration was part of what historians call the **Columbian Exchange**.

The other ingredients of a classic pizza also come from farther afield. Wheat was introduced from the Middle East. Basil was **indigenous** to the Indian subcontinent. And buffalo mozzarella was made from the milk of the water buffalo, an animal native to Asia.

So that classic "Italian" pizza? It wouldn't exist without ingredients from all over the globe.

[THE SLICE ON PIZZA]

In 1960, pizza cost 15 cents a slice.

Pizza began as a regional food, specific to Naples, Italy. In fact, Italian dictionaries from the late 1700s defined "pizza" as a type of **focaccia** bread found within the city. Fishermen would often fetch a pizza before setting out to sea, leading to its sauce to be called **marinara**, for seafarer. Over time, pizza evolved and changed, but it was never considered a fancy food. In fact, many wealthier residents and visitors in Naples looked down on it. Noted American inventor Samuel Morse traveled to Naples in 1831. He described pizza by saying it "altogether looks like a piece of bread that had been taken reeking out of the sewer."

Pizza dough must be rolled into a ball.

A chef spoons red tomato sauce on pizzas.

Pizza got its big break in 1889, when Italy's rulers King Umberto and Queen Margherita visited Naples. As legend goes, a few days into the trip, Queen Margherita grew tired of eating elaborate banquet foods. She asked for a sampling of local specialties. A **pizzaiolo** named Raffaele Esposito was assigned to make her three pies. The country had united just a little more than a decade before. Esposito made a dish that mirrored the new nation's red, white, and green flag. The local tomatoes, buffalo mozzarella, and basil wowed the queen. In her honor, it came to be known as the "Margherita pizza." And in the years that followed, it would travel across the ocean to a new place, where it was further changed and reimagined.

Italy wasn't a unified country until the second half of the 1800s. Different regions of the country had very different language and food traditions. Foods eaten in Italy's southern cities like Naples and Genoa were extremely different from those in places like Rome and Turin.

CHAPTER 2

Migrations

Between 1880 and 1930, about 4.6 million people immigrated from Italy to the United States. Many came from southern Italy, including Naples. In New York, Italian neighborhoods sprang up around the city. A large **enclave** settled into the cheap **tenement** apartments of Manhattan's Lower East Side. People called it "Little Italy." In this strange new place, people craved the comforts and tastes of home. It wasn't long before Gennaro Lombardi began serving pizzas to his fellow **expatriates**.

A photograph of Mulberry Street in Little Italy in 1900.

In 2016, 250 chefs gathered in Naples, Italy, and created the world's longest pizza at 6,082 feet (1,854 meters).

Lombardi came to New York in 1897 with the hopes of becoming a tailor. But the city already had enough tailors, so he entered the grocery business instead. His store at 53 ½ Spring Street in Little Italy began serving portable tomato pies similar to those in his native Naples. They were a hit, especially with workers. By 1905, Lombardi had shelved the dry goods and applied for a restaurant license. America's first pizzeria was born.

Pizza took a new shape and form in America, based on the ingredients and technology available. Spongy, soft buffalo mozzarella that was so important to Naples' signature Margherita pizza wasn't widely available in the United States. So chefs like Lombardi began

In the late 19th and early 20th centuries, economic opportunity drew Italian immigrants not just to the United States, but also to parts of South America. Between 1857 and 1940, Italians settled in particularly large numbers in Argentina. The country's first documented pizza was dished up in 1882 by native Neapolitan Nicholas Vaccarezza in Buenos Aires.

A calzone is like a portable pizza. It has all your favorite ingredients baked inside a pocket of dough.

experimenting with cow's milk products. Fresh, sun-ripened tomatoes like those found in southern Italy couldn't be found year-round in New York. As a result, canned tomatoes were imported from Italy. Other foods widely available in the United States, especially meats, got loaded onto the reinvented pies as toppings. Then, they were baked in coal-fired ovens, the American substitute for the blazing hot wood-fired ovens of Italy.

Wood-fired ovens only take about 1 to 2 minutes to cook a pizza.

Domino's® Pizza sells an average of 3 million pizzas daily.

For decades, pizza remained a neighborhood sensation in a few Northeastern states. It didn't catch on as a nationwide trend until after World War II. Soldiers who were stationed in southern Italy returned home with an appetite for the dish. Add more leisure time, an interest in dining out, and the desire for new and exotic foods, and pizza moved into the mainstream.

In the late 1950s and early 1960s, two Midwestern **franchises**, Pizza Hut® and Domino's® Pizza, set out to capitalize on Americans' growing taste for pizza. Offering home delivery and a standardized pizza, consumers knew exactly what to expect from these chains.

Pizza Hut® soon grew to a global empire, and Domino's® established a major foothold near college campuses and military bases. At the same time, pizza started to appear in frozen food aisles at grocery stores. Totino's® frozen pizzas, launched by Rose and Jim Totino in 1962, rocketed to coast-to-coast success in the second half of the century.

On the other side of the Atlantic Ocean, pizza was gaining a fan base outside of Naples, Italy. After World War II, many people migrated from the country's south to the more industrial north, bringing pizza with them. At the same time, tourists traveling to the country expected to find pizza on restaurant menus. In response, restaurants began offering menus that featured dishes from all of Italy's regions.

Pizza-making impostors are NOT welcome! In May 2004, the Italian government established a law to define and protect real Neapolitan pizza. The rules state the correct diameter, crust thickness, oven temperature, and ingredients for the pie. As stated by the pizza police, only tomatoes from San Marzano and buffalo mozzarella are to be used on authentic Neapolitan pizzas.

[THE SLICE ON PIZZA]

CHAPTER 3

Evolution and Wild Variations

Today, many chefs look at pizza as a blank slate for their own ideas. Of course, there are traditionalists who remain loyal to the time-honored pies of Naples, Italy. Still others create entirely new and zany varieties. Let's take a trip to see what you might get served in different corners of the globe.

Our journey starts in Naples, the probable birthplace of pizza. Grab a hand-formed, thin-crust pizza baked to perfection at 905 degrees Fahrenheit (485 degrees Celsius). There's no delivery option here—Neapolitan pizza must be eaten right away!

When enjoying pizza patatosa, you have the option of having your potatoes fried, baked, or mashed.

Have you ever faced the tough choice between pizza and french fries? Just hop on a ferry from Naples to the Mediterranean island of Sardinia. There, you don't have to choose one or the other. With pizza patatosa, you get both. French fries as a pizza topping is reported to be a huge hit with Sardinian kids and teens.

Next, zip east to Turkey or Armenia. Order up lahmacun, which is also spelled lahmajoun. This thin flatbread is served with minced meat, vegetables, and herbs. It's also spiced with cayenne, paprika, cumin, and cinnamon. But skip the cheese, which isn't standard on this Middle Eastern pie.

Ready to stretch your mind like a baker stretches dough? Venture across the Armenian border into neighboring Georgia. Try Adjaruli Khachapuri, a Georgian specialty that looks like an egg-filled pizza boat. Tear off some of the cheesy crust and dip it into the yolky egg for a filling meal.

Trek next to Japan for your next food adventure. Is it a pancake? Is it an omelet? Is it a pizza? It's **okonomiyaki**, a dish that gets its name from the sauce drizzled across its top! Often referred to as Japanese pizza, okonomiyaki's base is made of flour, grated yam,

Looking for a seriously local slice? In recent years, "pizza farms" have cropped up across the United States, particularly in the Midwestern states of Wisconsin and Minnesota. In the warmer months, guests enjoy pizza topped with farm-fresh ingredients outdoors, often in the company of grazing goats and hearty heifers.

Chicago-style deep dish pizza features the sauce on top of the toppings and cheese.

cabbage, egg, and water. Other ingredients, such as vegetables, fish, and cheese, are added to the mix and cooked on a stovetop. Top it off with Japanese mayonnaise, bonito flakes, and its namesake sauce.

Think pizza has to be circular? A journey across the ocean to Detroit, Michigan, will make you think again. The Motor City's thick-crusted, rectangular pizzas get their shape from the steel pans in which they're baked. Those pans weren't originally designed for pizza. They were actually used as automotive drip containers. Detroit-style pizza makers prefer Wisconsin brick cheese over mozzarella, which gives their pies a crispy, cheesy edge.

New York-style pizza is long and thin. Most New Yorkers fold their pizza when eating it.

No pizza tour is complete without a trip to New York City! Grab a giant slice at the legendary Lombardi's in Little Italy. Travel uptown to John's on Bleecker Street and to Totonno's on Coney Island for

> Over its long history, pizza has been twisted into knots and folded into sandwiches. But molded into a cone? That's fairly new. The Kono Company, founded in 2004, declared pizza reinvented with its hand-held, ice cream-inspired creation. At one of Kono's food trucks, you can get a classic cone filled with tomato sauce, mozzarella, and basil, or opt for a cannoli dessert cone.

more coal-fired deliciousness. Both restaurants were founded by chefs who cooked in Lombardi's famous ovens.

Our pizza journey ends in Buenos Aires, Argentina. While Neapolitan pizza was first introduced to Argentina in 1882, another style came by way of an immigrant from Genoa, Italy, in 1893. Called fugazzeta, this dish is like a traditional Italian focaccia bread stuffed with mozzarella. And by stuffed, we mean stuffed . . . a large pie contains an estimated 2 pounds (0.9 kilograms) of cheese!

May the Best Pizza Maker Win

Welcome to the World Pizza Games, a competition held each year at the International Pizza Expo in Las Vegas, Nevada! At this unique sporting event, pizzaiolos compete in Freestyle Acrobatic Dough Tossing, Fastest Dough, Largest Dough Stretch, Fastest Pizza Box Folding, and the Pizza Triathlon. What does a Pizza Triathlon include? Box-folding, fast dough, and large dough skills are all tested in the event, which contestants hope to finish in just under 40 seconds.

CHAPTER 4

Make Your Own!

In the ancient Middle East and Greece, pita bread topped with olive oil, herbs, and spices was frequently served as an "edible plate." Use the pita as a base to make your own pizza. Add any ingredients that you like—you can be traditional or think outside the box! After you've baked it, you decide—is your creation a pizza?

INGREDIENTS:

- Pita bread
- Olive oil
- Toppings of your choosing:
- For traditional Margherita pizza, tomatoes, mozzarella cheese, and basil are necessary.

Have an adult help you cut your different toppings.

DIRECTIONS:

1. With the help of an adult, preheat the oven to 400 degrees Fahrenheit (204 °C).
2. Place the pita on a cookie sheet and brush it with olive oil.
3. Get inspired by the offerings featured in chapter 3 and add toppings of your choosing!
4. Place pizza in the oven. Cook for 10 minutes.
5. Remove from the oven, let cool for 5 minutes, slice, and enjoy!

Pizza tastes best when it's shared!

10 Fascinating Facts, Best Served by the Slice

- In 2006, Joe Carlucci achieved history's highest recorded acrobatic dough toss at 21 feet, 5 inches (6.5 m).

- Frozen pizza is a hot business. More than 350 million tons are sold in the United States each year.

- The world's largest collection of pizza boxes belongs to Scott Wiener of Brooklyn, New York. He has more than 1,550 unique cardboard collectibles.

- Hawaiian pizza wasn't actually invented in Hawaii. It was first plated in 1962 by Sam Panopoulos in Chatham, Ontario, Canada.

- Think Americans gobble up the most pizza? Actually, Norwegians take the pie! Each resident of consumes about 11 pounds (5 kg) of pizza per year.

- While most pizzas at New York's Industry Kitchen cost less than $20, there's one exception. A pie topped with truffles, gold leaf, and caviar can be had for $2,700.

- Visit Philadelphia's Pizza Brain to see the world's largest collection of pizza-related items. While there, grab a slice of traditional or not-so-traditional pizza—brussels sprouts and brown sugar, anyone?

- In 2001, Pizza Hut® executives worked with Russian food scientists to deliver a pizza to the International Space Station.

- In 1977, the founder of Atari Video Games opened Pizza Time Theater in San Jose, California. Here, families ate pizza while watching a rocking band of robotic animals. Its name later changed to Chuck E. Cheese®.

- In late 2020, a French chef broke the Guinness World Record for the most types of cheese in a 12-inch (30 centimeter) pie. Benoît Bruel's creation boasted 254 distinct cheeses.

Timeline

1544 The first written reference to the tomato is in Italy.

1700s Italian dictionaries include a definition for "pizza."

1800s European and American travelers visiting Naples, Italy, comment on the city's food culture, including pizza.

1882 Pizza is reportedly first served in Buenos Aires, Argentina.

1889 In Naples, Raffaele Esposito prepares a pizza of tomatoes, mozzarella, and basil for Italy's king and queen. It is named the Margherita pizza in honor of the queen.

1905 Gennaro Lombardi opens his pizzeria at 53 ½ Spring Street in New York City, New York.

1958 The first Pizza Hut® opens in Wichita, Kansas.

1960 The first Domino's® Pizza opens in Ypsilanti, Michigan, near Eastern Michigan University.

1984 The True Neapolitan Pizza Association (Associazione Verace Pizza Napoletana) forms to protect and preserve Neapolitan-style pizza.

2001 Pizza Hut® delivers a pie to the International Space Station.

2004 Italy establishes a pizza law that defines and protects Neapolitan pizza.

Further Reading

BOOKS

Felix, Rebecca. *Rose Totino: Pizza Entrepreneur.* Minneapolis, MN: ABDO Publishing, 2018.

Martin, Claudia. *Pizza and Pasta.* Berkeley Heights, NJ: Enslow Publishers, 2019.

Sullivan, Jaclyn. *What's in Your Pizza?* New York, NY: PowerKids Press, 2012.

WEBSITES

MYSTERYdoug—Who Invented Pizza?
www.mysterydoug.com/mysteries/pizza
Watch this video to learn more about who invented pizza.

Wonderopolis—Who Invented Pizza?
www.wonderopolis.org/wonder/Who-Invented-Pizza
Check out this website to learn more about the invention of pizza.

GLOSSARY

Columbian Exchange (kuh-LUHM-bee-uhn eks-CHAYNJ) the transfer of plants, animals, technology, diseases, and culture between the Americas, West Africa, and Europe

early modern period (UR-lee MAH-duhrn PIHR-ee-uhd) the period of European history that roughly spans from 1450 to 1750

enclave (AHN-klayv) a cluster or group

expatriates (ek-SPAY-tree-ayts) people living outside the country of their birth

focaccia (foh-KAH-chee-uh) a type of flat, Italian bread often seasoned with herbs

franchises (FRAN-chizez) companies' licenses to individuals to own and operate their businesses

indigenous (in-DIH-juh-nuhss) native to a place or region

leavened (LEH-vuhnd) something made with yeast

marinara (mair-uh-NAIR-uh) a type of tomato sauce

Neapolitans (nee-uh-PAH-luh-tuhns) people from Naples, Italy

okonomiyaki (oh-kuh-now-mee-AH-kee) a sweet, tangy Japanese sauce; "pizza" in Japan is sometimes referred to by this name

pizzaiolo (PEET-suh-yoh-loh) a professional pizza maker

tenement (TEH-nuh-muhnt) a house divided into separate apartments

INDEX

Adjaruli Khachapuri, 22
Argentina, 15, 25, 30

basil, 7, 11, 30
buffalo mozzarella, 19.
   See also mozzarella cheese.

cheese, 7, 11, 15, 19, 23, 25, 29
Chicago, IL, 4, 23

Detroit, Michigan, 23
Domino's® Pizza, 18, 19, 30
dough, 9, 16, 25, 29

Esposito, Rafaele, 11, 30

focaccia bread, 8, 25
fugazzeta, 25

immigrants, 12, 15
Italy, 11, 12, 19, 30.
   See also Naples, Italy

Japan, 22-23

Kono Company, 24

"Little Italy," 12, 13, 15
Lombardi, Gennaro, 12, 15, 30

Margherita pizza, 11, 15, 30
marinara sauce, 8
milk products, 16
mozzarella cheese, 7, 11, 15, 19, 30

Naples, Italy, 6-8, 11, 12, 14, 15, 20, 30. See also Neapolitan pizza.
Neapolitan pizza, 7, 19, 20, 25, 30
New York City, New York, 12, 15, 24-25, 30

okonomiyaki, 22-23
ovens, 16, 17

pizza
   consumption, 29
   deep dish, 23
   dessert, 6
   early history, 4-6
   facts about, 29
   farms, 22
   frozen, 19, 29
   fruit, 6
   ingredients, 6, 7, 15-16, 23

New York-style, 24-25
overview, 4-11
records, 14, 29
restaurants, 15, 18-19, 24-25
spread of popularity, 12-19, 29
thick-crusted, 23
toppings, 5, 16
variations around the world, 20-25
Pizza Hut®, 18, 19, 29, 30
pizza patatosa, 21

recipe, 26-27

sauce. See tomatoes.

timeline, 30
tomatoes, 6, 7, 10, 11, 16, 19, 30
Totino's®, 19

wheat, 7
World Pizza Games, 25

32 [21ST CENTURY SKILLS LIBRARY]